View from the Hôtel de l'Etoile

poems by

Rebecca Manery

Finishing Line Press
Georgetown, Kentucky

View from the Hôtel de l'Etoile

Copyright © 2016 by Rebecca Manery
ISBN 978-1-63534-057-0 First Edition
All rights reserved under International and Pan-American Copyright Conventions.
No part of this book may be reproduced in any manner whatsoever without written permission from the publisher, except in the case of brief quotations embodied in critical articles and reviews.

ACKNOWLEDGMENTS

For my family, with love.

I would like to thank the editors of the following journals for their support in publishing earlier versions of some of the poems in this collection:

Rhino - "Goatherd"
The Body Politic - "Visions of Infinity in the Milwaukee Art Museum"
Bennington Review - "Playing Persephone," "Playing Desdemona," "Instructions for a Prestige (Famulus)," "Revision/Playing Daphne"
Inertia - "Plum Street, Detroit, 1967," "Dictionary Definition of Marian Anderson," "Playing Desdemona"

Publisher: Leah Maines

Editor: Christen Kincaid

Cover Art: Michiko Itatani, "Ascending Order" from Cosmic Theater AO-1, 2014. Used by permission of the artist. www.michikoitatani.com.

Author Photo: Rebecca Manery

Cover Design: Elizabeth Maines

Printed in the USA on acid-free paper.
Order online: www.finishinglinepress.com
  also available on amazon.com

Author inquiries and mail orders:
Finishing Line Press
P. O. Box 1626
Georgetown, Kentucky 40324
U. S. A.

Table of Contents

View from the Hôtel de l'Etoile 1

Playing Daphne 2

Instructions for a Famulus 3

Self-Portrait with White Rabbit 4

Sleight of Hand 5

Playing Persephone 6

Against Conjuring 7

Death of Mary with Cherubim and Moth 8

Hoodie 9

Blue Parrot 10

Goatherd 11

Mythologies 12

Unscripted Scene from a Processional Play 15

Pont Neuf, November 1999 16

The Look 17

Playing Desdemona 18

Desdemona Listens from the Next Room 19

Plum Street, Detroit, 1967 20

Dictionary Definition of Marian Anderson 21

Visions of Infinity in the Milwaukee Art Museum 22

Archeology of Deceit 23

History Lesson 24

Self-Portrait at the End of the World 25

Playing Penelope 26

Last Call at the Celestial Tap 27

Portrait with Former Planet 28

The Wish 29

Ars Poetica 30

Heavens, I'm spinning. And I use this verb as a planet would.

—Colette

View from the Hôtel de l'Etoile
after Joseph Cornell

Plenty of vacancies
but no porter.
You'll have to carry
your own luggage in.

Nothing in the lobby
but dusty glass,
a map and a moon
like a dull yellow ball.

Strange constellations
fleck the blue walls.
Hallways present
identical doors.

In the courtyard's
pale pavilion
a woman sits
covered in birds.

Stars continue
their inevitable drift.
In the room where you stand
it begins to snow.

Playing Daphne

It took a long time, that transformation.
She had to train hands to flower, fingers
to curl, then straighten again as leaves.

For a long time she remained between forms
firm trunk supporting fragile flesh.
It had to start with thought, the slow alchemy

of imagination pushing against matter
until they were the same. In this way
she attained a rare freedom.

Instructions for a Famulus

Be small and malleable. Have bones
that flex and bend, the better to fold
in his service. Drumrolls will greet
your appearance in feather headdress,
stilettos, flowing robe that declare
you're no small fry for swallowing.
Strip to your sequins for the trick, trip
the spring in the dark, make yourself
disposable. Head pressed to chest,
revel in the gasp that greets your
absence. Picture the bow your
Magician makes when they applaud.
Nothing to do now but wait it out
sequins pressing into your chin
till he lets you be substantial again.

Self-Portrait with White Rabbit

To fit
into this
garden I
need
to shrink.
Why fan
myself until I
can wear his
gloves? I
hate the
timid tick
of his pocket watch,
that absurd checkered waistcoat.
I want to love my large hands.

Sleight of Hand

Closed in fists or splayed like bird's feet
Hands will leave you holding the match.

Restless dexterity endlessly reaching, they are
monkey mind, tentacled flesh, understudies for ego.

Paired, they pray, applaud, pull rabbits
out of hats, skate the body's sidewalk.

Undercover, they circle throats, slither down alleys
like animate gloves, giddy in their crowns of nails.

This hand holding yours is a five-headed lie
that beckons, caresses—then waves goodbye.

Playing Persephone

A thirst for rubies will leave you in the dark.
Yellow leaves at your feet. Ginkgo.
In the morning you sit in a red chair
by a fireplace that's never known a chimney.
Forgetting the bones beneath.

Against Conjuring

A dead man makes a bad guest, ungrateful,
demanding. Before you waste

your words on prayers and spells to force
him back, consider what your false

desire creates: how he will linger
on a threshold he can't cross, how he will suffer

for the sake of passion he can't taste,
and how he will hate you for it, tossed

out of a quiet death into a living stream
that sickens him. You cannot tame

him to living. He will not, like a moth,
be drawn into your heat. In the cellar of his mouth

blood becomes rust. You'll hear your kindness cursed.
Let the dead stay dead. You cannot love a ghost.

Death of Mary with Cherubim and Moth

Brown moth squeezes into the picture frame
and is trapped at the bottom of the painted bed.
Flanked by angels with tinseled wings

it starves or suffocates in this imaginary room where
the merciful Mother of God quietly expires,

blonde hair flowing over the pillow while
bodiless cherubs float overhead, lips open to
serenade the dying Virgin, agonized moth

beating its body against the glass—
wild winged thing exempt from Ascension.

Hoodie

> *Indeed I will wed thee; a pretty creature is the hoodie.*
> —"The Hoodie-Crow"

She wants a lover and finds a crow.
Of course she thinks him enchanted.
She believes in the alchemy of love.

From the top of an ancient eucalyptus
he caws and bows, drops gifts
of bark and savory beetles.

She plucks out three golden hairs,
floats them up to him on the wind.
His feathers are mirrors. And remain.

Sometimes she is content to feel
his weight on her shoulder, see
his inquisitive eye fill up with her image.

Of course it can't last. Yet still
in dreams she finds herself wrapped
in the embrace of blue-black wings.

Blue Parrot

> *A crow will lead you to an empty barn, a parrot to sugar.*
> —Rumi

I'm a sucker for an empty barn—
plenty of shadows to hide in.
I've always followed the crow—

but yesterday I saw that parrot perched
like a waterfall, its body glowing like sapphires.

"You again," I said. "You
had me rushing off in moonlight,
digging for doubloons. You had me
pulling off my khakis, diving in
lagoons. You know what you can do

with your treasure map, your fabled pearl?"
All the while itching to finger
those hyacinth feathers.

Goatherd

The goats have eaten my hat and shoes.
My frock is mud-rimmed, my thistle-
bearing hair a haystack I search in vain.

I wade into the flock
take a young one in my arms
stroke the tender nubs of his horns

until he bleats.
In the next field a billy bellows.
The sea of she-goats tenses, gathers.

Mythologies
for PJ

> *I asked myself, "What is the myth you are living?" and I found that I did not know....*
> —C.G. Jung

1.

On the rooftop of a mountain
the most beautiful man in the world
sees his reflection in the setting sun.

Arms full of irises
he swoops down on the village
like prophecy fulfilled.
Overhead the sun spins
like a pinwheel.

His weeping stops clocks.
He crosses his arms against
his chest
cupping his shoulders
as if he can feel
wings growing.

2.

On a rooftop in Chicago
we turn our backs to the sky
and watch the sun set
on the mirrored face
of a curved grid of green glass.

In the twilight
object and reflection merge
testing our belief in vision.

The light rising from the city
embraces you like
a divine aura.

Your eyes burn
like the haunted eyes
of a wolf.

3.

You are Icarus flying
into the sun.
I am the mermaid
who cut out her tongue
for love of a man.

Hybrids of half-light
we never pause to wonder
whether we chose our myths or
were created by them.

4.

In this city by an inland sea you
burn with thirst
like a man wrapped in fever.

In a frozen landscape
I walk on bloodied feet
searching for love
like a lost limb.

Around me singed
feathers fall like
snow.

5.

You go to the wrestling place.
You are the man with burning eyes.
You are the angel
wings on your shoulders.
In the impartial desert
you struggle toward synthesis or
self-immolation.

6.

When the most beautiful man in the world cries
colors stream from his irises
and streak the desert like a sunset.

7.

Out of the burning sky
a man plunges into the ocean
his arms spread to embrace his reflection.

Under the waves
unseen
a woman reaches to receive him
her hair tangling his limbs
as she leads him down.

Unscripted Scene from a Processional Play

They go to see *Curious Beautiful* at the Neo-Futurarium above Nelson's Funeral Chapel. Halfway through the performance, they get ahead of the others and wander into a room draped with black curtains. The only light comes from three candelabra on a long table set with silver and china. Though it's a play about Vermeer, she's thinking of Calvino's *Castle of Crossed Destinies* and Cocteau's *La Bête*. They sit across from one another. They don't speak. He pats his jacket for cigarettes. She reaches into her pocket and pulls out the miniature Vermeers an actor had pressed into her palm in the last room. She centers Allegory of Painting on the plate in front of her, admiring the effect. She tucks *The Little Street* into the fold of a napkin, drops *The Girl with the Wineglass* into a wineglass, looks up to find him shaking his head. Last week when they crashed a wedding reception at the Palmer House he had twisted the heads off roses and strewn petals down the hall. She slides *Girl Asleep* under a knife. He stands up. Hearing a chair scrape, the actress in the next room leans her head on her palm, closes her eyes.

Pont Neuf, November 1999

Her mind is a reliquary for lost thoughts.
Through it floats a cold moon, heart
on a hill, Paris holding a river
between its luminous hands.

It was the cold end of an old century.
Looking down, hands cupping a match, he
didn't see the river catch her reflection
and the plate of the moon carry it away.

The Look
    after Le Fox Terrier du Pont des Arts, 1953 *by Robert Doisneau*

Qu'est-ce que tu fais?
the dog's eyes say.
In Paris, in winter
nude women linger
on every frigid bridge
for men to admire.
Dogs see nothing strange
in desire.

The men, oblivious, don't begin
to notice the famous Monsieur Doisneau.
The dog's his silent witness, though—
Dogs aren't so easily
taken in.

This dog's instantly aware.
Cautiously it sniffs the air
but smells no reason for alarm.
Voyeurs, it thinks, can do
no harm.

Fifty years have passed since then.
Of model, artist, and the man
who led his dog upon a chain
only images remain.
Doisneau has turned into a book.
Nothing lingers but
the look.

Playing Desdemona

She scans the cast and finds her name
in a dim hall outside the green room.
Music, soft as faded wallpaper, drifts
in from behind the stage door.

She puts the cup to her lips—

                my heart's subdu'd.

Imagines herself *a moth of peace.* Suddenly—
moths everywhere.

Desdemona Listens from the Next Room

Even without words, the sound of his voice could melt marble.
Alone in this distant room she can only imagine
what island of vipers, what two-backed beast, what treachery
he describes to her father, who is calling for more wine.

She's tired tonight. Under her needle, colored threads
tell their own story: ships lying fallow, a maid sacrificed,
a hero driven to murder, the snare of death catching
the king in his bath. A prick of pain: there's blood on the cloth.

Plum Street, Detroit, 1967

There was a bell around the neck
of the black man's blonde girlfriend.

They were hippies, wildflowers.
They moved like animals, like gods.

I saw a pale hand inside a dark one,
stripe of their coupled fingers.

I hadn't heard of napalm or Martin Luther King.
I had no word for the way they looked at each other.

I was sent away in July when the riots broke out. Too
late. The bell around my neck already ringing.

Dictionary Definition of Marian Anderson

Two dates, one photo,
a word and a half:

Amer. contralto.

The rest left out to
conserve space.

Visions of Infinity in the Milwaukee Art Museum
after Josiah McElheny's Modernity circa 1952, Mirrored and Reflected Infinitely

inside a glass box
mirrored jars stretch
to infinity

a disembodied eye
i recognize
as mine

hovers like a green sun
or the eye of god
on a dollar bill

over emptiness
and reflections of
emptiness

weeks before
the bailout
will begin

Archeology of Deceit

A lie is like a dinosaur bone. One edge is protruding, making a bump in the smooth terrain. You stub your toe a number of times and finally get curious. So you dig, and out comes a jaw bone. Then you're worried, because you know where there's a jaw there must be a skull, spine, pelvis, rib cage, all the rest. Suddenly you're no longer on familiar territory. A shadow is cast over the ground you thought you knew, the shadow of a dinosaur of immense proportions. You divine the placement of the bones beneath the surface. You can see them as if you'd x-rayed the earth. The geography has shifted, as if the bones had rumbled. You can never forget the bones. You can feel them in your own.

History Lesson

The sound of oars echo against
peeling frescoes. Reflected water
sways over the domed ceiling
where sparrows roost in chandeliers.
We can almost hear the statues
collapsing into sediment.

                        Cameras flash.
The guide spins the expected narrative.
When we dock at the grand staircase
minds numb with royal names and dates
of reigns, only a child asks, "The ones
who worked here, where did they go?"

Self-Portrait at the End of the World

Today: Flash floods, changing to snow.
Tomorrow: Chance of Horsemen.
Through hurricanes, elections, invasions,
I've kept my nose buried in a book.

It's not that I don't care. I recycle,
support public schools. I don't drive
an SUV or wear fur. Twice, I swear,
angels have used my body for higher

purposes. Still, I can't decide whether
I'd be a beer drinker or a car washer in
the Sheryl Crow song. Even at the end
of the world, I don't know how to have fun.

Playing Penelope

We were out of gas and millionaires.
The water was undrinkable so
our thirst was unquenchable. Every
morning we walked the former roads
to the only jobs left. All day
we built walls—out of concrete,
out of stone, out of mud. At night
we tore the walls down to keep
employment high, to let our lovers
in. What else could we have done
while waiting for a hero to save us?

Last Call at the Celestial Tap

They've worked a 10-eon day
in the explosives factory
and now they're worn out, falling apart.

The stars constellate at the bar,
swap stories of better eras when they
stayed out all night, crept home at first light.

Who could have predicted they'd be relegated
to this neutrino heap in a peripheral suburb?
The bartender pours sympathy, wipes

the counter down as the stars nod over their drinks.
Already their centers are collapsing.
Already they have forgotten who they are.

Portrait with Former Planet

We've always been camera-shy, you and I, but now
that we're used to demotion why not smile? You're
an exhibitionist, exposing your heart, your dark spots.
There I am, as always a little out of focus. The ideas
they had about us: honeymooners of the underworld,
or a spectral ferryman and a gloomy king. We're just
detritus now.

I've never been photogenic. Those red eyes, that blank look
are not all there is to me. You, me, these other floating
rocks—we're tendrilled somehow. Once the camera's gone
we can go back to being majestic.

The Wish

And what would you wish for
little dreamer, little boathook
if you had that fish on your line?

Bread enough for carp and goose and all—
bread without fighting.

And what would you wish for yourself
little stumbler, little planet
as you wobble through your orbit?

Let there be a lap to lay my head in
before the end of my wanderings.

What if the fish refuses
weeping willow, keening bell?

Fish who gives what can't be kept—
let me not live silent under water.

Ars Poetica

The jagged glass
I threw into the lake
one bitter afternoon
has returned, carried
on the backs of many waves.

But notice the transformation:
Rounded, smoothed,
opaque as silk.
It fits in my palm
like a talisman.

Notes

Page 1 "View from the Hôtel de l'Etoile" was inspired by a series of Joseph Cornell boxes (including Untitled (Hôtel de l'Etoile), 1954) formerly displayed together in Room 237D of the Art Institute of Chicago.

Page 2 In the original myth, Daphne is changed into a laurel tree by her father after she begs him to save her from being raped by Apollo. In this version, Daphne performs her own gradual transformation.

Page 3 "Instructions for a Famulus": A famulus is a "servant or attendant, especially of a scholar or a magician" (dictionary.com).

Page 9 "Hoodie": The epigraph is from "The Hoodie-Crow," a Scottish fairy tale in *The Lilac Fairy Book* edited by Andrew Lang (Dover, 1966/1910).

Page 15 "Unscripted Scene from a Processional Play": *Curious Beautiful,* Conor Kalista and Rachel Claff's processional play based on the life and works of the 17th Century Dutch painter, Johannes Vermeer, premiered at Chicago's Neo-Futurarium in September of 2000.

Page 18 "Playing Desdemona": Lines in italics are from Shakespeare's *Othello*.

Page 21 "Dictionary Definition of Marian Anderson": In 1939, the Daughters of the American Revolution refused to allow the celebrated African American contralto, Marian Anderson, to sing for an integrated audience in Constitution Hall. Instead, Ms. Anderson performed on the steps of the Lincoln Memorial for a crowd of over 75,000. These facts are not mentioned in the minimalist entry for Marian Anderson in the third edition of the *American Heritage Dictionary*.

Page 24 "History Lesson" was inspired by a phrase from John Ashbery's blurb for Andrew Zawacki's *Anabranch* (Wesleyan University Press, 2004): "...like being rowed along the corridors of a flooded palace."

Page 26 "Playing Penelope": In Homer's *Odyssey*, Penelope, wife of the long-absent Odysseus, stalls her impatient suitors by saying she will choose another husband once she has finished weaving her father-in-law's burial shroud. She weaves by day, but undoes her work by night.

Page 28 "Portrait with Former Planet": On July 14, 2015, NASA's New Horizons spacecraft captured high resolution images of Pluto and its moon, Charon.

Additional Acknowledgements

Thanks to Leah Maines, Christen Kincaid, and the other fine folks at Finishing Line Press for their faith and support in publishing this first book.

Grateful thanks and appreciation to Michiko Itatani for permission to use a reproduction of her painting, "Ascending Order" from *Cosmic Theater AO-1*, 2014, on the cover. Find more work by this extraordinary artist at www.michikoitatini.com.

Thanks to the talented teachers and students I have worked with at Bennington Writing Seminars and the University of Michigan, especially Amy Gerstler, Major Jackson, Timothy Liu, Ed Ochester, Michael Burkard, Liam Rector, Laura Kasischke, Keith Taylor, A. Van Jordan, and Petra Kuppers. Thanks also to Jane Hirshfield and the Napa Valley Writer's Conference; Rosellen Brown, Melanie Braverman, and the Spoleto Arts Symposia; Reginald Gibbons; Diane Wakoski; and Debi Richardson, wherever you are. To my Chicago crew, especially Karen and Phil Parrillo, April Nauman, Cathryn "Bula" Bulicek, Mark Shanabrough, Melissa Lindbergh, Drew Martin, Paul Mack, and all of my former co-workers at The Center. To Kathy Edgren and theresa rohlk, *les salonistes extraordinaires*, and the UUAA Community of Writers. To Nancy Harrower and Dr. William Darmody, my first literary teachers. Most of all to my family: Charles and Patricia Manery, Beth and Jeff Gleason, Chip and Michelle Manery and their children, grandchildren, and great-grandchildren: present, in memory, and still to come.

Rebecca Manery is Assistant Professor of English at Ball State University. She holds a Ph.D. in English and Education from the University of Michigan, an MFA in Creative Writing from Bennington College, an MA in Literacy Education from Northeastern Illinois University, and a BA in English from Michigan State University. She has taught undergraduate courses in creative writing and composition at the University of Michigan, graduate and undergraduate courses in literacy education at Northeastern Illinois University, professional development workshops for the Chicago Teachers' Center, and a continuing education course on the plays of the Court Theatre season at the University of Chicago. She has also served as an Arts in Education Director, dramaturg, teacher, and writer for numerous professional theatres and theatre-related organizations in New York City and Chicago including New Dramatists, Pan Asian Repertory Theatre, A.R.T/New York, Court Theatre, Stage Left Theatre, Chicago Dramatists, the Theatre Department of Loyola University of Chicago, Steppenwolf Theatre and Chicago Shakespeare Theater. Her research on creative writing pedagogy has been published in *New Writing: The International Journal for the Practice and Theory of Creative Writing*. With Stephanie Vanderslice, she is the editor of the forthcoming 10th anniversary edition of *Can Creative Writing Really Be Taught? Resisting Lore in Creative Writing Pedagogy* from Bloomsbury Press. A passionate believer that creative writing and other arts are fundamental human practices, she has founded and facilitated community workshops to support the development of writers of all ages.

www.ingramcontent.com/pod-product-compliance
Lightning Source LLC
LaVergne TN
LVHW041504070426
835507LV00012B/1327